LEVEL
1

Spiders

Laura Marsh

NATIONAL
GEOGRAPHIC
Washington, D.C.

For the students, teachers, and staff at Edgewood School —L.F.M.

Design by Yay Design

Trade paperback ISBN: 978-1-4263-0851-2
Library binding ISBN: 978-1-4263-0852-9

Photo credits: Cover, Brenda Blakely/ National Geographic Your Shot; 1, Gerry Ellis/ Digital Vision/ NationalGeographicStock.com; 2, Ingo Arndt/ naturepl.com; 4, Maneesh Kaul/ National Geographic My Shot; 5, iStockphoto.com; 6, Merkushev Vasiliy/ Shutterstock; 7, Francis Quintana/ National Geographic My Shot ; 8, Roy Escala/ National Geographic My Shot ; 9, Zohar Izenberg/ National Geographic My Shot ; 10, Cathy Keifer/ Shutterstock; 11, Oxford Scientific/ Getty Images; 12 (bottom), iStockphoto.com; 12-13 (right), Greg Harold/ Auscape/ Minden Pictures; 14, Joel Sartore/NationalGeographicStock.com; 15, Amy Ambrose/ National Geographic My Shot ; 16, Radhoose/ Shutterstock; 17 (top), Natural Selection/ Design Pics/ Corbis; 17 (center), Arco Images GmbH/ Alamy; 17 (bottom), Hans Christoph Kappel/ naturepl.com; 19, Tara Blackmore/ National Geographic My Shot ; 20, Gerry Pearce/ Alamy; 21 (top), Ocean/ Corbis; 21 (bottom), John Cancalosi/ NationalGeographicStock.com; 22 (top), David Haynes/ Alamy; 22 (bottom), Bach/ Corbis; 23 (top), M. Kuntner; 23 (bottom), Danita Delimont/ Alamy; 24, Emanuel Biggi/ Getty Images ; 25 (top), Premaphotos/ Alamy; 25 (center), Darlyne A. Murawski/ NationalGeographicStock.com; 25 (bottom left), Geoff du Feu/ Alamy; 25 (bottom right), iStockphoto.com; 26-27, Stephen Dalton/ naturepl.com; 28, Karen Zieff/ www.zieffphoto.com; 29, Panoramic Images/ Getty Images; 30 (left), Radhoose/ Shutterstock; 30 (right), Audrey Snider-Bell/ Shutterstock; 31 (top left), Flickr RF/ Getty Images; 31 (top right), Kjell Sandved/ Visuals Unlimited/ Corbis; 31 (bottom left), Brian Nolan/ iStockphoto.com; 31 (bottom right), Photoshot Holdings Ltd/ Alamy; 32 (top left), Emanuel Biggi/ Getty Images; 32 (top right), Photoshot Holdings Ltd/ Alamy; 32 (bottom left), Oxford Scientific/ Getty Images; 32 (bottom right), John Cancalosi/ NationalGeographicStock.com.

Printed in China

15/RRDS/3

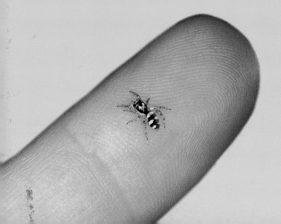

Table of Contents

It's a Spider!

What has eight legs, fangs, and hair all over?

Is it a monster? No. It's a spider!

Some of us are afraid of creepy-crawly spiders.

But most spiders can't hurt people.

Web Word

FANG:
A biting mouthpart of a spider or a large, sharp tooth in other animals

Spiders, Spiders Everywhere!

Spiders live in deserts and rain forests. They live on mountains and plains.

They live on beaches and in caves. Spiders live almost anywhere.

A Spider's Body

Spiders can
be big or small.
They can be
brown or black.

Some spiders
are red, orange,
green, or yellow!

abdomen

Abdomen?
Say *AB-doh-men*

head

They may come in different colors.
But all spiders have eight legs. And
they all have two main body parts—
a head and an abdomen.

Spider Food

spider

insect

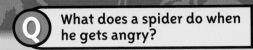
All spiders are meat–eaters.
Most spiders eat insects.

Some spiders eat bigger animals like fish, snakes, lizards, or frogs.

Sometimes spiders even eat each other!

spider

frog

11

Spiders have fangs that hold venom.
Venom kills the prey or keeps it
from moving.

But spiders don't
have teeth to chew
their food.

They suck the
liquids out
of their prey.
Yummy!

Web Word

VENOM: Poison
PREY: An animal
that is eaten by
other animals

fangs

Senses

Most spiders have eight eyes.
But they can't see very well.

So they need more than their eyes
to catch dinner.

Small hairs on a spider's legs sense movement. A spider feels an insect caught in its web. It's dinnertime!

Web Builders

orb web

Different spiders make different webs. Orb webs have a circle pattern.

funnel web

Funnel webs are built like tubes.

tangle web

Tangle webs (cobwebs) are a jumble of threads.

trap-door spider's web

Trap-door spider webs cover a spider's home in the ground.

Spinning Silk

Not all spiders make webs. But all spiders make silk.

They wrap their eggs in silk. They wrap their prey in silk, too.

Spiders even travel by silk! They use it like a rope. Spiders climb down to different places. Or they let the wind carry them.

A spider wrapping its prey in silk

Super Spiders!

Check out these really cool spiders from all over the world.

Strangest

Bolas spider
It catches its prey with sticky thread, as if fishing.

Goliath birdeater tarantula

It's so big, it can eat young birds. It lives in South America.

Biggest

Most Famous

Black widow

It is the most poisonous spider in North America. It sometimes eats its mate.

Brazilian wandering spider

It shows its red jaws when angry. It lives in South and Central America.

Deadliest

Best Leaper

Jumping spider

It stalks its prey. It leaps huge distances to pounce on its lunch.

Darwin's bark spider
It makes the world's largest webs—as big as two city buses!

Best Weaver

Best Mother

Wolf spider
She's a fierce predator but a careful mother. She carries her babies on her back!

Baby Spiders

Big or small, all spiders start out as eggs. A mother spider protects her eggs in an egg sac.

eggs

egg sac

Some spiders lay up to 2,000 eggs.

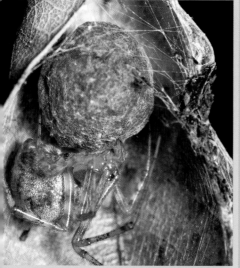

She may keep the egg sac safe on a web, under a leaf, or in a log.

She may carry her egg sac with her, too.

Web Word

EGG SAC:
A silk pouch that protects and holds spider eggs

The spider eggs hatch!

Baby spiders crawl out to meet the world. They are called spiderlings.

27

Helpful Spiders

Spiders are helpful to have around.

Their silk is super strong. It's light and stretchy. People are finding new ways to use spider silk.

Fabric made from spider silk

Spiders also eat biting bugs such as mosquitoes.

Let's hear it for spiders! Hooray!

What in the World?

These pictures show close-up views of spidery things. Use the hints below to figure out what's in the pictures. Answers on page 31.

HINT: This is a usual spider hangout.

HINT: If you had eight of these, you could do many things at once!

3

HINT: More of these don't help spiders. Our two work better.

4

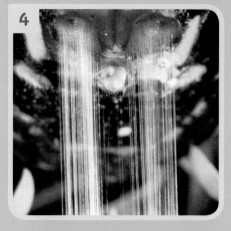

HINT: Spiders don't drink milk. But they make something that rhymes with it.

5

HINT: Rock-a-bye-baby... Spiders' eggs are kept safe in this.

6

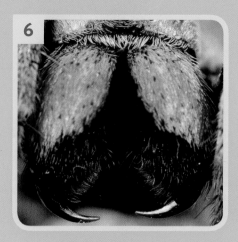

HINT: Ouch! These can give a nasty bite.

Answers: 1. web, 2. legs, 3. eyes, 4. silk, 5. egg sac, 6. fangs

Glossary

EGG SAC: A silk pouch that protects and holds spider eggs

FANG: A biting mouthpart of a spider or a large, sharp tooth in other animals

PREY: An animal that is eaten by other animals

VENOM: Poison

LEVEL
2

Sharks!

Anne Schreiber

**NATIONAL
GEOGRAPHIC**

Washington, D.C.

To Ben, who taught me to love unlovable animals.
—A.S.

Published by the National Geographic Society, Washington, D.C. 20036. All rights reserved.
Reproduction in whole or in part without written permission of the publisher is strictly prohibited.

Schreiber, Anne.
Sharks! / by Anne Schreiber.
p. cm. — (National Geographic readers)
ISBN 978-1-4263-0286-2 (paperback) — ISBN 978-1-4263-0288-6 (library binding)
1. Sharks--Juvenile literature. I. Title.
QL638.9.S292 2008
597.3—dc22
2007044161

Cover: © Tim Davis/CORBIS; Title Page: © Jeffrey L. Rotman/Getty Images; 2-3: © Gary Bell/
Oceanwidelmages.com; 4-5: © David Fleetham/Mira/drr.net; 6(inset), 18(bottom, right):
© Shutterstock; 6-7, 11, 32(top, left): © Mark Conlin/V&W/Image Quest Marine; 7(inset), 18(middle),
19(top), 32(bottom, left): © Bob Cranston/SeaPics.com; 8-9, 18(top), 18(bottom, left), 32(bottom, right):
© Doug Perrine/SeaPics.com; 10: © Niall Benvie/Nature Picture Library; 12-13, 22(bottom), 32(center,
both): © Masa Ushioda/SeaPics.com; 14-15: © Kike Calvo/V&W/Image Quest Marine; 16-17, 19(bottom),
32(top, right): © Jeff Rotman/SeaPics.com; 20-21: © David Doubilet/National Geographic Image
Collection; 22(top): © James D. Watt/SeaPics.com; 22-23 (ribbon illustration): © Photodisc/Getty
Images; 23 (both): © C&M Fallows/SeaPics.com; 24-25: © Espen Rekdal/SeaPics.com; 26-27:
© Gary Bell/SeaPics.com; 28: © Steve Robertson/ASP/Covered Images/Getty Images; 29:
© Noah Hamilton Photography; 30-31: © David D. Fleetham/SeaPics.com.

Table of Contents

CHOMP!

What is quick?
What is quiet?
What has five rows of teeth?
What glides through the water?
CHOMP!
It's a shark!

Sharks live in all of Earth's oceans.
They have been here for a long time.
Sharks were here before dinosaurs.

OCEANIC WHITETIP SHARK

CARTILAGE: Cartilage is light, strong, and rubbery. The tip of your nose is cartilage. Can you feel how soft it is?

Shark tail fins are larger on top. This helps them move through the water better.

HAMMERHEAD SHARK

A shark is a fish. But a shark is not like other fish. Sharks do not have bones. They have soft cartilage instead. Cartilage helps sharks twist and turn. Cartilage helps sharks move and bend.

If a shark loses a tooth, a new one moves forward to take its place.

Shark skin feels bumpy and rough. It's hard like sandpaper. It protects sharks and helps them swim faster.

Shark Pups

Shark babies are called pups. Some pups grow inside their mothers. Other pups hatch from eggs.

LEMON SHARK

Lemon shark pups grow inside their mothers. The lemon shark mother goes to shallow water to give birth. The pups stay near the shallow water until they are grown.

These fish are called remoras. They hang around sharks and eat their leftovers.

LEMON SHARK PUP

9

MERMAID'S PURSE

Swell shark pups hatch from eggs. The mother sharks lay the eggs in hard cases. People call the case a mermaid's purse.

A pup coming out of its egg case.

SWELL SHARK PUP

Swell shark mothers lay up to five egg cases at a time. In nine months, the swell shark pups are born.

Pups Grow Up

NURSE SHARK

WORD BITES

PREDATORS: Animals that eat other animals.
PREY: Animals that are eaten by other animals.

When shark pups grow up, they are awesome predators. They have many ways to sense their prey. Did you know a shark can smell blood from miles away? It can smell one drop of blood in 25 million drops of ocean.

Sharks can see better than humans can. Even in deep, dark water, a shark can see its prey.

Sharks take a test bite of prey before eating. Their taste buds tell them if the prey is fat enough to eat.

GREAT WHITE SHARK

What Big TEETH You Have

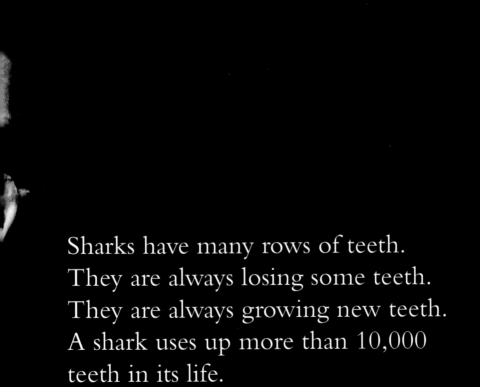

Sharks have many rows of teeth.
They are always losing some teeth.
They are always growing new teeth.
A shark uses up more than 10,000
teeth in its life.

Different sharks have different teeth.
Their teeth are perfect for what they eat.

Long, spiky teeth are
for catching.

Flat teeth are for
grinding.

Serrated teeth are
for ripping.

WORD BITES

SERRATED: When something is serrated,
it has a jagged edge, like a saw blade.

18

PREHISTORIC: Prehistoric is a time before people wrote things down.
EXTINCT: Extinct plants and animals are no longer alive on Earth.

MEGALODON TOOTH

Wow! Prehistoric sharks had really big teeth—up to six inches! Good thing these guys are extinct.

The megalodon is a prehistoric shark. Scientists made a life-sized model of the megalodon's jaw and put in the teeth they have found. You can imagine how big the shark must have been.

Imagine This!

A giant shark is gliding through
the water.
A swimmer is nearby.
The shark gets closer.
It is huge.
It opens its giant mouth and…

WHALE SHARK

…sucks in a big mouthful of water.
The swimmer is fine.
The shark is a whale shark.
Whale sharks are the biggest sharks.
But they have tiny teeth.
They eat tiny animals called plankton.

Blue-Ribbon Sharks

There are about 375 different types of sharks

WEIRDEST
The Hammerhead Shark

A hammerhead shark has a head shaped like a giant hammer. Its wide head is great for hunting.

The spined pygmy shark is about eight inches long. It has a glow-in-the-dark belly.

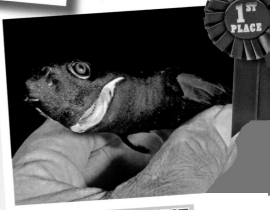

SMALLEST
The Spined Pygmy Shark

When a great white bites its prey, its eyes roll back into its head. This protects its eyes.

CREEPIEST
The Great White Shark

The mako is the fastest shark. It can swim up to 20 miles per hour. Makos leap clear out of the water to catch prey.

FASTEST
The Mako Shark

Now You See Them...

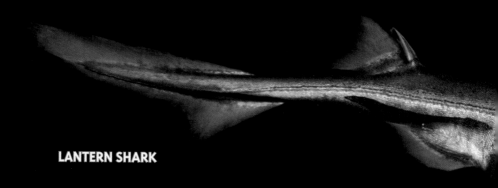

LANTERN SHARK

Some sharks glow in the dark! Do you see something shiny in the water? Watch out! The tiny lantern shark is covered with a glow-in-the-dark slime.

The lantern shark is a deep-sea shark. Many deep-sea animals glow. Scientists think glowing might help predators attract prey.

Most sharks are hard to see. They have a dark back. From above, they blend in with the water. They have a white belly. From below, they blend in with the sky.

WOBBEGONG SHARK

Some sharks have special ways to hide.
Wobbegongs have colors like the seafloor.
Their mouths have parts that look
like seaweed. Fish swim in but they can't
get out!

Shark Attack!

One day Bethany Hamilton went surfing. Suddenly, a tiger shark attacked. It tugged her as she held onto her surfboard. It took a big bite out of her surfboard. It also took Bethany's left arm.

After the attack, Bethany wanted to keep surfing. She is not afraid to go in the water. She knows that shark attacks are rare.

Bethany says, "One thing hasn't changed — and that's how I feel when I'm riding a wave."

People Attack?

Shark attacks are scary, and terrible. Sharks can be a danger to people. But people are a bigger danger to sharks. Millions of sharks die in nets set to catch other fish. Others are killed on purpose.

Many types of sharks may become extinct. Sharks have been on Earth for millions of years. Sharks and people need to learn to share the sea.

GRAY REEF SHARK

CARTILAGE
Cartilage is light, strong and rubbery. Shark skeletons are made of cartilage.

EXTINCT
Extinct plants and animals are no longer alive on Earth.

PREDATOR
A predator is an animal that eats other animals.

PREY
Prey are animals that are eaten by other animals.

PREHISTORIC
Prehistoric is a time before people wrote things down.

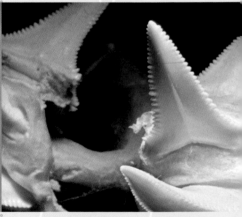

SERRATED
When something is serrated, it has a jagged edge.

LEVEL
2

Tigers

Laura Marsh

**NATIONAL
GEOGRAPHIC**

Washington, D.C.

For Claire and Ellie
—L. F. M.

Design by YAY! Design

Library of Congress Cataloging-in-Publication Data
Marsh, Laura F.
National Geographic readers. Tigers / by Laura Marsh. — 1st ed.
p. cm.
ISBN 978-1-4263-0911-3 (pbk. : alk. paper) — ISBN 978-1-4263-0912-0 (library binding : alk. paper)
1. Tiger. I. Title.
QL737.C23M2748 2012
599.756—dc23
2011035282

Cover, Gerry Ellis/Minden Pictures; 1, Martin Harvey/Corbis; 2, Eric Isselée/Shutterstock; 4, Ron Kimball/Kimball Stock; 6
DLILLC/Corbis; 6 (bottom), Terry Whittaker/FLPA; 7, Tom and Pat Leeson/Kimball Stock; 8 (top), Michael Nichols/Nationa
graphicStock.com; 8 (center), Andyworks/iStockphoto.com; 8 (bottom), Mike Liu/iStockphoto.com; 9 (top), Matthew
iStockphoto.com; 9 (top, center), Daniel Cox/Photolibrary RM/Getty Images; 9 (bottom, center), Fuse/Getty Images; 9
tom), Dimitar Marinov/iStockphoto.com; 10, Wild Bill Melton/Corbis; 11, Anup Shah/naturepl.com; 13, Digital Vision/Get
ages; 14 (top), PhotoDisc; 14 (center), Dirk Freder/iStockphoto.com; 14 (bottom), Jens Klingebiel/iStockphoto.com; 15
left), Michael Nichols/NationalGeographicStock.com; 15 (top, right), Schalke fotografie/Melissa Schalke/Shutterstock; 15
tom, left), Michael Nichols/NationalGeographicStock.com; 15 (bottom, right), Tiago Estima/iStockphoto.com; 16, Eric Is
Shutterstock; 17, Ocean/Corbis; 18 (top), Ocean/Corbis; 18 (bottom), Michael Nichols/NationalGeographicStock.com; 19,
Lynn/Corbis; 20, Steve Bloom Images/Alamy; 21 (top), DLILLC/Corbis; 21 (bottom), Lynn M. Stone/naturepl.com; 22-23, Ge
lis/Minden Pictures; 27, Savigny/npl/Minden Pictures; 28, Terry Whittaker/Frank Lane Picture Agency/Corbis; 30 (top), D
Vision; 30 (center), Ingo Arndt/Minden Pictures; 30 (bottom), Suzan Charnock/iStockphoto.com; 31 (top left), Michael
ols/NationalGeographicStock.com; 31 (top right), Martin Ruegner/Getty Images; 31 (bottom, left), drbimages/iStockph
com; 31 (bottom, right), M. Robbemont/Shutterstock; 32 (top, left), Michael Nichols/NationalGeographicStock.com; 32
right), Gerry Ellis/Minden Pictures; 32 (left, center), Franco Tempesta; 32 (right, center), Galyna Andrushko/Shuttersto
(bottom, left), Schafer & Hill/Getty Images; 32 (bottom, right), Theo Allofs/Minden Pictures/NationalGeographicStock

Table of Contents

PURR-fectly Big Cats

Bengal Tiger

Q On which side does a tiger have the most stripes?

A The outside!

Tigers are big and beautiful animals. They are strong and powerful, too. Tigers are the biggest cats in the world.

A Tiger's Home

Tigers live in the forest. They spend a lot of time in the water, too. They live in hot places like Indonesia. They live in cold places like Russia.

Indochinese Tiger

Siberian Tiger

Tigers that live in cold places are bigger than other tigers. They also have thicker fur to keep them warm.

Built for Hunting

Tigers are fierce hunters. Their bodies are built for catching prey.

Coat

A tiger's stripes camouflage it in tall grass and dry leaves. Its prey may not see the tiger until it's too late.

Teeth

Four large teeth help tigers kill prey quickly.

Eyes

A tiger's terrific eyesight helps it hunt at night.

Q What do you get when you cross a tiger with a sheep?

A A striped sweater!

Paws

Big paws with soft pads help a tiger walk quietly. Sharp claws hook into prey and don't let go.

Tail

A long tail helps a tiger keep its balance when moving quickly.

Back legs

Big muscles help a tiger dash or leap at its prey.

Tiger Term

CAMOUFLAGE: An animal's natural color or form that blends in with what is around it

PREY: An animal that is eaten by another animal

Meat Eater

Tigers are carnivores, animals that eat meat. Their favorite foods are large, hooved animals such as buffalo, deer, and wild pigs.

A hungry tiger can chow down 80 pounds of meat in one meal. That's about 320 hamburgers!

Tiger Turf

Besides hunting, tigers spend a lot of time marking their territory. They are not good at sharing!

Tigers make long scratch marks on trees. They also rub their faces on trees and leave smelly scents. This tells other tigers to stay away.

Tiger Term

TERRITORY: An area that an animal protects from other animals

Siberian Tiger

Cool Cat Facts

Check out these neat facts about tigers.

No two tigers have exactly the same stripes.

Whiskers help a tiger feel its way in the dark.

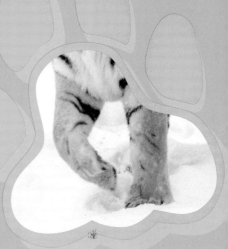

Large paws keep Siberian tigers from sinking in deep snow.

Tigers can live in temperatures as low as -40 degrees Fahrenheit.

Tigers are great swimmers. They are never far from water.

A tiger's front teeth are three inches long.

Tigers have much better hearing than humans.

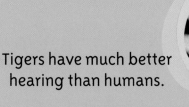

Cubs

A female tiger usually has two or three cubs at one time. The cubs weigh about four pounds at birth.

The mother raises the cubs by herself. Male and female tigers come together only to have cubs. Otherwise, adult tigers live alone.

Bengal Tiger

17

A mother Bengal tiger nurses her young.

The cubs drink their mother's milk. After three or four months, they start to eat meat.

Tiger cubs play games. They chase, leap, and pounce. They are learning how to be good hunters. When they are two years old, young tigers leave their family to find their own territories.

Tiger Talents

Tigers are full-grown when they leave their families. They are big, heavy cats, but they can climb trees and jump great distances.

Bengal Tiger

In fact, tigers can leap as far as 30 feet. That's as long as five adult men lying head to toe!

And, unlike house cats, tigers are good swimmers. They like to cool off in rivers and pools.

Sumatran Tiger

The White Tiger

The white Bengal tiger is very rare. It can't grow orange fur. Its white coat, brown stripes, and icy blue eyes are quite a sight.

You won't find a white Bengal tiger in the wild. But you might be able to see one in a zoo.

White Bengal Tiger

23

Tigers in Trouble

Asia

South China
Tiger

Bengal
Tiger

Indochinese
Tiger

Indian Ocean

Where tigers
used to live

Where tigers
live today

Sumatran
Tiger

Tigers are endangered. About 100 year

ago, there were 100,000 tigers in the

wild. Today there are less than 3,500.

Pacific Ocean

There are five different kinds of tigers today. They are the Bengal (BEN-gol), South China, Indochinese (in-doh-chi-NEEZ), Sumatran (soo-MAH-truhn), and Siberian (si-BEER-ee-uhn) tiger. Three other kinds of tigers have already become extinct.

Tiger Term

ENDANGERED: At risk of dying out

EXTINCT: A group of animals no longer living

Why are tigers disappearing?

Tigers are losing their habitat. People cut down trees. Tigers live and find food in the forests. When forests disappear, so do tigers.

People also kill tigers for their body parts. Their skins are used for rugs. Other parts are used to make traditional Chinese medicines.

Killing tigers is against the law. But it still happens today.

Tiger Term

HABITAT: The place where a plant or animal naturally lives

Q What do you get when you cross a tiger with a snowman?

A Frostbite!

South China Tiger

Helping Tigers

Bengal Tiger

Though tigers are in trouble, there is good news. New forest areas for tigers have been found. Also, people are planting trees where forests have been cut down.

You can help, too. Tell your family and friends about what you've learned. We can all work together to keep tigers on our planet!

Stump Your Parents

Can your parents answer these questions about tigers? You might know more than they do!

Answers at bottom of page 31.

1

How do tigers spend their time?

A. Howling
B. Hunting and marking their territory
C. Sharing their territory
D. Eating plants

2

What is special about a tiger's paws?

A. They are small but powerful
B. They don't sink in deep snow
C. They have three toes
D. They make noise when walking

3

How do tigers live?

A. Alone, except when a mother is raising her young
B. In groups of three to four
C. In groups of five to eight
D. With all their friends

4

What's important about a tiger's striped coat?

A. It sticks out
B. Its pattern is the same as other tigers'
C. It comes in many colors
D. It camouflages the tiger

5

What do tigers like to eat?

A. Fruits and berries
B. Insects
C. Meat — and lots of it!
D. People

6

Where do tigers like to live?

A. In the desert
B. Near water
C. In the mountains
D. On the savanna

What is a baby tiger called?

A. A pup
B. A kit
C. A cub
D. A gosling

7

CAMOUFLAGE: An animal's natural color or form that blends in with what is around it

ENDANGERED: At risk of dying out

EXTINCT: A group of animals no longer living

HABITAT: The place where a plant or animal naturally lives

PREY: An animal that is eaten by another animal

TERRITORY: An area that an animal protects from other animals

Wolves

Laura Marsh

NATIONAL
GEOGRAPHIC

Washington, D.C.

For Bonnie
—L. F. M.

All wolves pictured are gray wolves, unless otherwise noted.

Library of Congress Cataloging-in-Publication Data
Marsh, Laura F.
National Geographic readers. Wolves / by Laura Marsh.—1st ed.
p. cm.
ISBN 978-1-4263-0913-7 (pbk. : alk. paper)—ISBN 978-1-4263-0914-4 (library binding : alk. paper)
1. Wolves. I. Title.
QL737.C22M36423 2012
599.77—dc23
2011035283

Cover, Altrendo Nature/Altrendo RR/Getty Images; 1, Lynn M. Stone/Kimball Stock; 2, Tom Leeson/NationalGeograph Stock.com; 4–5, Digital Vision; 6, Jim Brandenburg/NationalGeographicStock.com; 7 (top), Wildlife GmbH/www.kimba stock.com; 7 (center), Zerlina Chen/Your Shot/NationalGeographicStock.com; 7 (bottom), Ana Gram/Shutterstock; 8 (A Eric Isselée/iStockphoto.com; 8 (B), Joel Sartore/NationalGeographicStock.com; 8 (C), Roy Toft/NationalGeographicStoc .com; 8 (D), Ann and Steve Toon/Robert Harding/Getty Images; 8 (E), lifeonwhite.com/iStockphoto.com; 8 (bottom), Vale rii Kaliuzhnyi/iStockphoto.com; 9 (left), Stanisław Pytel/iStockphoto.com; 9 (right), Joseph Van Os/The Image Bank/Gett Images; 10 (top), Kimball Stock; 10 (bottom), Lisa A. Svara/Shutterstock; 12–13, E. A. Janes/SuperStock; 14–15, Joel Sartore NationalGeographicStock.com; 17, Corbis Flirt/Alamy; 19, Jacqueline Crivello/Your Shot/NationalGeographicStock.com 20–21, John Pitcher/iStockphoto.com; 20, Jim Brandenburg/Minden Pictures; 22, Robert Harding World Imagery/Gett Images; 23, Picture Press/Alamy; 24 (top left), First Light/Getty Images; 24 (top right), Fedor Kondratenko/iStockphot .com; 24 (bottom left), iStockphoto.com; 24 (bottom right), Images in the Wild/iStockphoto.com; 25 (top left), Dar Egidi/iStockphoto.com; 25 (top right), Jim Brandenburg/Minden Pictures; 25 (bottom left), Marcia Straub/iStockphot .com; 25 (bottom right), Digital Vision; 26, Rolf Hicker/photolibrary.com; 27, Jean-Edouard Rozey/Shutterstock; 28–2 Joel Sartore/NationalGeographicStock.com; 30 (top), Galyna Andrushko/Shutterstock; 30 (center), Tammy Wolfe/iStocl photo.com; 30 (bottom), J-E ROZEY/iStockphoto.com; 31 (top left), Paolo Capelli/National Geographic My Shot/Nationa GeographicStock.com; 31 (top right), Joel Sartore/NationalGeographicStock.com; 31 (bottom left), Acilo/iStockphoto.com 31 (bottom right), Marek Brzezinski/iStockphoto.com; 32 (top left), Jacqueline Crivello/Your Shot/ NationalGeograph Stock.com; 32 (top right), Jim Brandenburg/Minden Pictures; 32 (left center), Stanisław Pytel/iStockphoto.com; 32 (righ center), Franco Tempesta; 32 (bottom left), Design Pics Inc./Alamy; 32 (bottom right), Jeff Lepore/Photo Researchers, In

Table of Contents

What's That Sound?

Arrooooooo!

There's a lonely howl in the distance. Then more voices join in. The chorus of howls sends a shiver down your spine.

What's making this spooky sound?

Wolves!

Wolves All Around

Wolves are found all over the world. They live in hot places like deserts. They also live in cold places like the North Pole.

The most common wolf is the gray wolf.

There are more than 30 kinds of gray wolves. And they are not just gray. They are brown, black, tan, and white, too.

Iberian Wolf

Arctic Wolf

Timber Wolf

7

Wolves and Dogs

Wolves are the largest members of the dog family. Foxes, coyotes, jackals, wild dogs, and domestic dogs are also members of this family.

Red fox

Coyote

Jackal

Wild dog

Domestic dog

Wolf

German Shepherd

Timber Wolf

Our pet dogs are relatives of the gray wolf. That's why they look alike.

Word bite

DOMESTIC: Tame and kept by humans

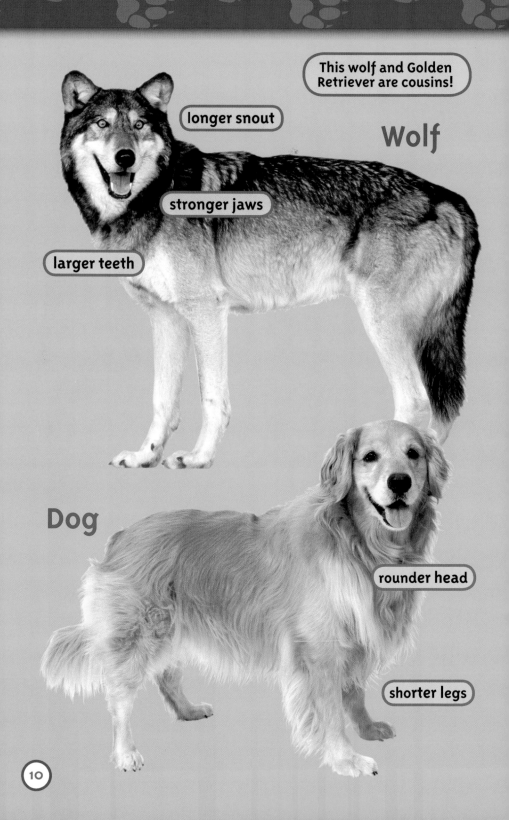

This wolf and Golden Retriever are cousins!

longer snout

Wolf

stronger jaws

larger teeth

Dog

rounder head

shorter legs

But wolves and dogs are different in several ways.

Wolves have a longer snout, stronger jaws, and larger teeth. Dogs have a rounder head and shorter legs.

The biggest difference is that dogs like to be around people, and wolves would rather be around other wolves.

Pack Life

Wolves live in family groups called packs. A pack includes a male and female wolf, their young, and a few wolves that have joined from other packs.

There are usually six to ten wolves in a pack.

Wolves need each other. Together they find food, protect one another, and care for their young. A wolf alone can't survive for long.

Hunting

Wolves are great hunters. They travel many miles without getting tired. They can usually run faster than their prey.

Wolves eat small animals such as rabbits. They also eat big animals such as moose, deer, caribou, elk, and bison.

And wolves eat a lot. They can each eat 20 pounds of meat in one meal. That's about 200 hot dogs!

Word bite

PREY: An animal that is eaten by another animal

Wolf Talk

How do wolves "talk" to the other wolves in their pack? They whimper, bark, growl, and snarl.

But when they need to talk long distance, wolves howl. And when one wolf starts howling, others tend to join in.

Howling is what wolves are famous for!

Leaders of the Pack

The pack's leaders are called alpha wolves. There is one alpha male and one alpha female in each pack. They are the smartest and best hunters.

Alpha wolves guide the pack. They decide when to stop hunting and where to sleep at night. Alpha wolves also eat first at every meal.

Word bite

ALPHA: A leader in a group

An alpha wolf lays its nose on top of a pack member's nose to show who's boss.

Pups

Baby wolves are called pups. Four to six pups are usually born in each litter.

Pups weigh one pound at birth and can't see or hear. They snuggle safely in their den with their mother for the first two weeks.

Every day they grow bigger and stronger. At about three weeks old, the pups leave the den to explore.

Word bite

LITTER: A group of animals born at one time

DEN: A hidden place in a cave or underground where animals live

When the pups are bigger, other wolves in the pack care for them, too. They bring the pups food. They also babysit them while the rest of the pack is hunting.

Wolf pups start hunting with the pack when they are six months old. When young wolves are two to three years old, they leave to form their own packs.

8 Wolf Wonders

1
Pups open their eyes when they are about two weeks old.

2
A wolf's sense of smell is about 100 times greater than a human's sense of smell.

3
Newborn pups can't keep themselves warm. They need mom for body heat.

4
Each wolf has its own howl, which sounds different from the howl of other wolves.

5

Wolves usually won't hunt outside their own hunting grounds.

6

Pups play with "toys" such as a small dead animal from a kill, or a piece of its bone or fur.

7

An alpha wolf shows who's boss by walking tall with its tail and ears held high.

8

Wolves roam long distances — as far as 12 miles in one day!

Fewer Wolves

Wolves rarely attack people. They are afraid of them. But wolves do attack farm animals. Mostly for this reason, people have killed millions of wolves. So many wolves were killed that there were no longer any wolves in a lot of places.

Furs of wolves killed by hunters

Today there are about 100 red wolves living in the wild.

Some people worried that wolves might become extinct. So they decided to help. They passed laws to protect wolves. Today wolves are returning to many places around the world.

Word bite

EXTINCT: A group of animals no longer living

27

Wolves Return

Wolves have returned to Yellowstone National Park. Once the park had many wolves. But only one wolf was left by 1926.

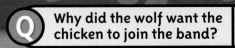

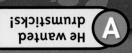

Scientists brought wolves from Canada into Yellowstone in 1995. The wolves had pups.

Now there are about 100 wolves in Yellowstone. Once again wolves make their home in the park.

Stump Your Parents

Can your parents answer these questions about wolves? You might know more than they do!

Answers at bottom of page 31.

1

Where do wolves live?

A. In the desert
B. In the mountains
C. In the forest
D. All of the above

2

Wolves like to "talk" long distance to one another by _____ .

A. Chirping
B. Squealing
C. Howling
D. Buzzing

3

What is the most common kind of wolf?

A. Red wolf
B. Gray wolf
C. Italian wolf
D. Werewolf